The Sacred
Choral Music of J.S. Bach

—A Handbook

Edited by Dr. John Butt

PARACLETE PRESS
Brewster, Massachusetts

Library of Congress Cataloging-in-Publication Data

   The sacred choral music of J.S. Bach : a handbook / edited by John
  Butt.
       p. cm.
  Includes bibliographical references.
  ISBN 1-55725-197-5 (pbk.)
   1. Bach, Johann Sebastian, 1685–1750—Choral music.
  2. Choral music—Instruction and study. 3. Choral singing—
  Interpretation (Phrasing, dynamics, etc.) I. Butt, John.
  ML410.B13S23   1997
  782.2'4'092—dc21

                                          97-29730
                                             CIP

10 9 8 7 6 5 4 3 2 1

Published by Paraclete Press
Brewster, Massachusetts
Printed in the United States of America

Foreword

This handbook is the fruit of many years of labor on the part of a number of people. Above all, the authors wish to acknowledge the contribution of the members of *Gloriæ Dei Cantores* and their director, Elizabeth Patterson. Coming from greatly varied musical backgrounds, they have shared a unique commitment: to bring to life the "vision" inherent in the great sacred music of the past and of our own time. Their ecumenical outlook, spirituality and discipline have made it possible for them to approach and learn the music of Johann Sebastian Bach, beginning with the most basic elements of vocal technique and musical expression.

Some of the information offered in this handbook was first presented to the registrants of the *Master Schola*, an annual music symposium held on Cape Cod with *Gloriæ Dei Cantores* as the resident choir. The subject was Bach and the aim was to provide church musicians, choir directors and organists, not only with significant aspects of recent research, but also to provide a systematic approach to the Bach repertoire—an approach which, we believe, is sensitive to the technical demands and spiritual implications of the music, and which can be applied successfully with inexperienced performers.

The Bach Schola mentioned above culminated in a performance of **Saint Matthew Passion**, which accounts for the references in the following pages to *Master Schola* and the **Passion**.

In the end, it is our hope and intent that this handbook assist choir members, directors, congregations, and indeed, all interested persons in their study, performance and enjoyment of Bach's sacred choral music.

Table of Contents

Historical Perspective & Introduction

Dr. John Butt

Today we know Bach to be one of the greatest composers of the entire Western tradition, one whose intense devotion to his liturgy and church was fortuitously matched by surpassing musical genius. Nevertheless, his reputation was gained many years after his death and the awe with which he is held today would have been almost incomprehensible to him and his contemporaries.

It is certainly true that Luther valued music as the second most important human activity after religion itself. Yet it is by no means the case that Luther's associates and followers shared this attitude. Throughout the seventeenth and early eighteenth centuries there was great dispute within Lutheran circles as to the value of music. What actually did it do? And did it add to or detract from the recitation of Scripture? How many secular elements were acceptable and how could operatic conventions be employed in a religious environment? Although most clerics would tolerate music in the severe style of the sixteenth century (it should not be forgotten that Luther's favorite composer was Josquin) the influence of the latest Italian styles, throughout the Baroque period, was greeted with both enthusiasm and censure. The orthodox viewpoint was to place music in the category of *adiaphora*—those things that neither added nor took away from the essentials of religious practice. In other words, music was considered something rather more neutral than many modern commentators suppose, but something that also conveniently preserved the art from the more negative views of the Calvinists (if it was technically impossible to prove that music was a positive spiritual force, one could at least claim that it did no harm). Church music of the most elaborate kind could indeed flourish in a private court chapel, such as Weimar (something that could not happen in the Pietist-influenced Mühlhausen, where Bach had previously worked). Leipzig, as a center of orthodox Lutheranism, was more likely than most cities to accept a musician who believed that the very best contemporary styles should be harnessed by the liturgy. Yet even here there was continual opposition—some tolerated the complex music only because it added lustre to a modern, commercial city; others found Bach's music unacceptable for serious church devotion. The position of music in the school was under constant threat from Enlightenment principles, which saw value only in "relevant," up-to-date subjects.

In short, attitudes towards the value of music and the place of music within religion were almost as varied as they seem to be today. For every contemporary who cherished the union of sacred and secular music, the complex and dramatic exegesis that Bach's music could provide, there was someone who promoted the strict separation of the sacred from the earthly realm and who advocated the simple recitation of the Word of God, free from liturgical condiments. The tide against elaborate church music and the rapid decline of the Lutheran musical establishments was well under way by the time of Bach's death and, at the end of the eighteenth century, church music had become one of the least important areas of musical culture in Lutheran Germany.

Ironically, Bach's reputation was made almost entirely within the secularized culture of absolute music during the early nineteenth century. After all, it was impossible to label a composer a "genius" before the advent of the cult of genius; it was likewise impossible to consider a piece of music as a "masterwork" before there was a notion of such an object. All Bach's major religious works were first heard by a wide public in the environment of the concert hall. Yet it would be a mistake to call this an entirely secular context. Just as there were people in Bach's time who saw the sacred in the best of secular arts (thus accounting for Bach's rewriting of secular pieces for sacred occasions, and his use of Italian and French secular idioms), the concert tradition of the nineteenth century gained much of its mystique through a sacralization of the musical experience. Music which pointed towards ultimate perfection, which seemed to encapsulate notions of supreme unity and coherence touched the religious sensibility of the nineteenth century. Indeed it could be argued that the religious depth of Bach's music was more appreciated by the secular concert public of the nineteenth century than it was by the congregations of his own time. Ironically Bach's music has been seldom heard (other than in mutilated extracts) in a religious environment during much of the nineteenth and twentieth centuries—the texts have often been seen as doctrinally suspect, and certainly limited; the pieces are often too long for modern liturgies and are often thought to appeal only to an elite section of the congregation. Without a lively culture of amateur performance, the pieces are too expensive to promote.

Today, at the end of the twentieth century, Bach's music can play a wider role in worship. Since the Second World War there has been a growing culture of "restoration," something most clearly evidenced in architectural reconstructions and renovations (particularly in war-torn Europe). Many things from the past are carefully preserved and "cleansed" of anachronism. In music, this is most obvious in the vogue towards "historically informed" performance—the interest in ancient instruments, early versions of current instruments and forms of performance practice that are no longer part of traditional modern practice. The "restoration" culture was not strong enough by the early 1960s to preserve the Roman Church from liturgical decline, but more recently there have been many moves towards restoring ancient liturgies and their attendent spiritualities. The moves towards greater ethnic and cultural diversity, particularly in the United States, may also have played a part in making many more receptive to seemingly remote liturgical practices. Bach's music, having earned much of its religious depth during the nineteenth century, is now an attractive prospect for many church and community choirs. Its difficulties in performance are indeed enormous, but with a systematic approach, sensitive to the technical demands and spiritual implications of the music, much can be achieved with inexperienced performers. Indeed those without a conventional "classical" training may be at an advantage in learning to sing the florid coloratura that many have seen as too "instrumental." This volume presents a wonderful opportunity to learn many of the basics of Bach performance and understanding. It will be of tremendous value to those who direct choirs and to those who sing and play.

Some Observations on Singing Bach

Dr. Craig Timberlake

INTRODUCTION

From the voice teacher's perspective, building a Bach choir and training a Bach singer are one and the same endeavor. As Christoph Wolff makes clear in *The New Grove*, the composer's vocal parts are cast in a seemingly instrumental idiom. He demands equivalent virtuosity from instrumentalists and singers. There are no concessions. The result, as Wolff notes, is a homogeneous musical language of considerable density.

What about the poetic language of the text? Henry S. Drinker, who in the early forties generously gave us four volumes of uncopyrighted English translations of the choral works, quoted the musicologist Hugo Leichtentritt's searing indictment of Bach's cantata poets:

> In all English and French literature of the past five hundred years hardly anything can be found to equal the poetry of the Bach cantatas in ponderousness, in bad taste, in inartistic exaggeration, and in diction devoid of all poetic grace and beauty. Nothing less than Bach's gigantic genius could have created out of these poor and repulsive verses music of the highest type.

Leichtentritt may have gone too far in his blanket condemnation, but Drinker in his essay from *On Translating Bach Texts* (Volume I), and in the overall quality of his effort, makes the case for American choirs singing Bach in English. As he noted, concerning the private printing and distribution of his translations, "Nothing is copyrighted, and amateurs, professionals and publishers are welcome to take, use and improve anything that they wish." So far as I know, this splendid offer still stands. Take the time and effort to seek out and study his contribution. (Please refer to this book's chapter, "Thoughts on English Translations in Bach's Vocal Works," for more specific assistance in obtaining English translations.)

Not to denigrate Drinker's devoted service to the ideal of singing Bach in English, when *Gloriæ Dei Cantores (GDC)* began the on-going study of Bach five years ago, we accepted the musical challenge of becoming choristers and soloists, as required, and the linguistic challenge of singing in Bach's native tongue, not ours. We began with the study and performance of the motets and then added selected cantatas, the *Mass in B-Minor* and the *St. Matthew Passion*. It did not take us long to discover that Bach demands from choral singers and soloists the same extraordinary levels of musicianship and vocal technique. Whether or not one agrees with the conclusion of the distinguished Bach scholar Joshua Rifkin to have a single voice per part, it is clear that the great cantor's choristers and soloists were indivisible. All of us, given our disparate vocal, musical, linguistic, and research skills, have joined in the effort to improve our individual awareness and competence. To be sure, the results of such a mutual endeavor have been uneven, but in the atmosphere of *Master Schola*, with its distinguished faculty and experienced staff, we were encouraged to present some topical considerations and strategies which have served our effort to date—to sing and play well with spiritual awareness, this most remarkable repertoire of sacred music.

TRAINING THE BACH SINGER

"Let the florid music praise." Setting aside for a moment basic vocal technique or natural ability, it is clear that for one to deserve the title of "Bach Singer," that person must command the florid style—that is, the ability to sing and phrase lengthy melismatic passages with the precision and color of a fine string or wind player. In approaching Bach it is never too early to begin the acquisition of coloratura flexibility through the working range of each category: soprano, alto, tenor and bass. In Bach, unlike Handel, the demands are basically the same for each voice type and hardly differentiated within a prevailing polyphonic style, except in such obvious matters as range and tessitura. At the end of this commentary you will find exercises derived from the Bach repertoire being studied by GDC, which became for a time, if not all time, a sort of "daily dozen" of exercises for each of our singers who had helped contribute to the list for their voice category. To conclude a singer's workout, such vocalises should be practiced slowly and evenly on the indicated vowels and gradually speeded up—[♩=60] andante, moderato to allegro [♩=120].

Choir members were divided into chamber groups, one voice on each part. They were free to indulge in whatever games or strategies might contribute to progress in the development of vocal flexibility, while maintaining a well-supported tone and adhering to the chosen tempo. In "grooving" these passages of running sixteenth notes at the cerebral and glottal level, singers may resort to various articulations (staccato, marcato, martellato) and/or the use of nonsense syllables, as in "swingling" (Ward Swingle) or "scatting" à la Ella Fitzgerald. Ehmann and Haasemann (Hinshaw,1981) offer other relevant exercises in their book, *Voice Building for Choirs*.

International Phonetic Alphabet (IPA)

Ehmann and Hassemann utilize the symbols of the IPA to insure correct pronunciation, enunciation and articulation in the practice of their exercises. The use of the IPA is now so pervasive in vocal pedagogy (See Miller, 1986 and 1993; McKinney, 1994 and Odom, 1981) that to keep up with significant contributions to the literature church musicians and other voice professionals should learn to read and transcribe phonetically. Good bilingual paperback dictionaries often carry IPA transcriptions in both languages, making them very useful aids to the singer who has acquired a working knowledge of the IPA symbols. Years ago, when I was teaching German lyric diction, one could buy Langenscheidt's German/English, for less than a dollar. Today the market is virtually glutted with expensive volumes which feature IPA and are aimed at the vocal-choral music educator.

At the end of this commentary you will find three pages of IPA symbols offering English, German, Italian and French equivalents of the sound represented by each symbol. These pages with accompanying lectures on application constituted *Gloriæ Dei Cantores'* first exposure to the IPA as a tool for singers and choir directors. This undertaking proved its worth in a Bach workshop, in our rehearsals of the *St. Matthew Passion* and in a German language recording of Brahms and Mendelssohn. You will find other sources in the selected readings given below. *The Phonetic Alphabet* (Cartier and Todaro, 1983) is a workbook which helps the singer effortlessly develop skills in a broad phonetic transcription. *German for Singers* (Odom, 1981) also offers exercises in transcription and pronunciation. Although designed for a three-hour university course, it is a useful reference for the Bach singer. Theodor Siebs' *Deutsche Bühnenaussprache-Hochsprache* has long been an authoritative source for German actors, singers and announcers. Kenyon and Knott's *A Pronouncing Dictionary of American English* provides a phonetic transcription of what is often vaguely called standard speech. Finally, a valuable recent edition is *International Phonetic Alphabet for Singers* (Wall, 1989).

VOICE TEACHING IN THE CHORAL CONTEXT

Bach is not the first or last church musician to be accused of neglecting his duties as a singing teacher. Such a genius can scarcely be blamed for turning over to prefects the task of training untalented, indifferent or hostile boys of the Thomasschule. He was, however, well trained as a singer in his boyhood and perfectly happy to teach a thirteen or fourteen-year-old with "a good strong voice and fine proficiency," particularly since a well-cultivated, unchanged voice in his day might continue until seventeen or eighteen.

Native endowment is one thing, a good ear another; but one cannot sing Bach by ear. What did Bach mean by a "fine proficiency"? Surely the student's acquired musical skills figured prominently in such an evaluation by Bach. Some years ago, when I first began to work intermittently with members of GDC, I became aware that their membership in the choir was contingent upon the successful completion of some eight books of music theory. In singing sacred choral music encompassing five centuries and a variety of historical styles and traditions and a number of languages, they were among the most challenged singers I have ever encountered. My first task was to assist the basses in continuing and maintaining a convincing Russian Orthodox sound in Old Slavonic, a language I could only approach phonetically. By employing Strohbass, glottal fry and an *ad hoc* combination of dark timbre, low laryngeal position and vowel modification in the critical lower range, we were able to augment briefly the genuine sonority of our one basso profondo and fulfill our concert commitments—even be reviewed as fine "Russian" basses. Such temporary measures pose considerable risks, however, just as they do when at the other end female singers are asked to sing with straight tone and "white voice" to satisfy an Early Music practitioner's notion of "period" sound. It is imperative not to interfere with the emergence of normal vibrato in a well-trained singer; i.e., vibrato which does not call attention to itself but is a concomitant of true *bel canto*. The challenge of the choir director and/or designated vocal surrogate is like that of the physician—to do no harm.

PEDAGOGICAL RESOURCES

During the several years of my association with GDC, I have been writing a regular column entitled *Practica Musicae* for the *Journal of Singing*, official organ of the National Association of Teachers of Singing. GDC singers are often in my mind when I address topics in pedagogy or performance practice. Several of these brief essays are listed in the selected readings given below. Often they attempt to reconcile for teacher and singer pedagogical perspectives of the past and present. Other columnists in the *Journal* are among today's leading investigators and commentators on historical and current scientific literature as it pertains to singing. Choir directors interested in expanding their knowledge of current writings on singing are encouraged to subscribe to the *Journal* or borrow it from a NATS member or a public or institutional library.

Most volumes on singing—and there is a substantial increase in the number of useful texts now in print—consider major topics under the four rubrics, Respiration, Phonation, Resonation and Articulation. James C. McKinney's new edition of his "manual for teachers of singing and choir directors," *The Diagnosis and Correction of Vocal Faults,* is indispensable. Two volumes by Richard Miller, *The Structure of Singing* (1986) and *Training Tenor Voices* (1993), are also essential reading for the choir director. Taken together, these three volumes will help the church musician not trained as a vocalist to approach such seemingly arcane topics as breath management, registers, articulation and vowel modification.

In the past, GDC members have been assigned readings to enhance their knowledge of physiology and anatomy relative to the human voice. They have been paired as teacher and student and served as critics of interpretation and performance in repertoire classes. Choral directors who have not done so might consider the possibilities of peer-mediated instruction. The chamber concept is a useful place to begin. Singing and playing Bach, Rifkin style—one voice or instrument on a part—can be highly instructive.

BACH'S RECITATIVO

Inspired by the Mozart Bicentennial celebration and the musical hubbub which marked the season of 1991–1992, I wrote two columns on Mozart's *secco recitativo* in his Italian operas. What Edward J. Dent wrote in his critical study of Mozart's operas (1913) is now more widely understood—that *recitativo secco*, "although apparently conventional and monotonous to the last degree, is as good a test as any of the merits both of poet and composer." Not only in opera but in sacred music, recitative is pervasive in the repertoire and an essential aspect to be addressed in the training of the singer.

Ideally, singers whose native tongue is English should first study Bach's recitative in a good English translation (Drinker). It expedites comprehension of recitative conventions and formulas and facilitates the acquisition of a particular character's conventional voice, as well as timbral changes (color) suggested by changing emotional states. Appropriate word accentuation, the irregular rhythms characteristic of the style, and changes in stress, articulation and rate of utterance, again related to character, are more easily acquired through the use of one's first language.

In English there are also lovely excerpts of *secco* for all voices in the sacred and dramatic music of Purcell and Handel. Dent overstated the case when he said that *secco* "may be seen at its worst in Handel's operas written for the London stage, the composer knowing full well that nobody would pay the least attention to it." There are some highly expressive *secco* recitatives in the operas and oratorios, not to mention the cantatas. Dent is right on target, however, with the observation that Handel's Italian recitatives, whether good or bad, "must be sung at the same pace as an actor would speak the words in a play without music." He adds:

> Handel adopted the same formulae in his English oratorios, and we may without hesitation lay down the same rule, that the *secco* recitatives in these must be sung no slower than the words would be spoken by a good reciter. It is, of course, equally evident that the same rule must be followed in Bach's Passions.
>
> (Dent, *Mozart's Operas,* p.64-66)

Another Handel authority, Paul Henry Lang, illuminates Handelian recitative in his splendid study, *George Frideric Handel* (see p. 612-615). He notes that the composer's Italian and English recitative satisfied expectations in their approximation of so-called "natural speech." Lang rails against a "solemn churchly delivery" in the oratorios, in which distortion is compounded when the organ serves as continuo. "Handel," he writes, "could be perfunctory, but he usually followed the requirements of the text, carefully planning his modulations and keeping the harmony moving to avoid the sort of turgidity our singers create artificially."

Bach, like Handel, may follow passages of *secco* with *stromentato (accompagnato)*. In fact, the suppleness and variety of Bach's recitative in the Passions and Cantatas is one of the miracles in the polarity of Baroque recitative and aria. How subtly and flexibly he moves from *secco* to *accompagnato* to *arioso* to *aria*. His biographer Spitta's brief comments on "Bach's Treatment of Recitative" should be read by every singer who would master the extraordinary expressivity of this German recitative.

BAROQUE PITCH

Nikolaus Harnoncourt has been a major contributor to my fuller understanding of so-called "authentic" performance of Bach's Passions and Cantatas. So far as I know, he has not chosen to rationalize A-415, or any other pitch level in his splendid recorded legacy, now happily available on CDs. His first recording of *St. Matthew Passion* with David Willcocks and King's College Chapel forces and soprano soloists from the Wiener Knabenchor remains one of my favorites at lower pitch.

The vexed questions surrounding Baroque pitch have been illuminated by two recent commentaries: 1) the essay by Cary Karp on "Pitch," Chapter VII, The *Norton-Grove Handbooks,* (Vol. 2, *Performance Practice: Music after 1600*) and 2) *The New Grove* article on "Pitch," with particular attention to numbers 2-5, by J.J.K. Rhodes and W.R. Thomas. In view of the wide concern expressed here and in Europe over the ever-rising pitch level, teachers and students might read these sources for a useful historical perspective. A number of singers and instrumentalists have supported the noted tenor Carlo Bergonzi in calling for a lower pitch standard, C=256 Hz (about A=430). C=256 was put forward in 1713 by Joseph Sauveur, and according to Karp, remains in use as "physical" or "scientific" pitch. I have found Bergonzi's public demonstrations persuasive from both the physiological and aesthetic points of view. We would do well to heed his assertion that future generations of singers are at risk in a world of rising pitch. As an aspect of performance practice, pitch level has received considerable attention. Perhaps commercial reasons, such as the marketing of musical instruments, dictated the identification of a "correct" Baroque pitch of A=415.3 Hz. As Rhodes and Thomas point out, recently manufactured keyboards now have a device for shifting the keyboard to the left by a semitone "so that instead of A=440 the pitch level approximates to A=415.3 (equivalent to B♭=440 in equal temperament)." For most modern practitioners, say our authors, this seems in some respects a feasible compromise between the chamber pitch levels they discuss.

For the voice teacher or choir director, working with individual voices, it can be highly instructive to transpose recitatives and continuo arias up or down a semitone in search of optimum quality and ease of production. In the discovery and growth process, one should enjoy singing Bach and be made as comfortable as possible while doing so. Transposition, as someone once said, was invented by singers and should be freely applied to attain maximum artistic results.

BEL CANTO

What Did Bach Know and When Did He Know It?

Albert Schweitzer in his biography of the composer tells us that, "unfortunately, we have no means whatever, of learning how Bach taught singing." He cautions us not to rate too high or too low the performances of Bach's schoolboys. He reminds us that "the technique of singing was at that time a more general possession than it is now. Colorature [sic] and trills were practiced even in the elementary stage of instruction, and anyone who possessed the least natural aptitude for singing could soon acquire a certain, though maybe a superficial facility. . . . Possibly his scholars sang the arias better from a technical point of view, than we might expect. . . ."

Schweitzer notwithstanding, it is tempting to suggest that Bach didn't teach singing at all, but rather taught music to these youngsters, because there was little time to do anything else. As another biographer, Spitta, points out, "Bach required of his singers, in the first place, accuracy of pitch and time, a pure intonation, fertility of resources, and also, if possible, a pleasing quality of voice—*eine feine Stimme*." Given the limitations of time—seven hours of singing a week with as many as forty participants in the Thomasschule, Bach's educational philosophy, simply stated, must have been above all the "education of the gifted" in order to meet the demand for serviceable choir singers.

Bach himself had been a well-regarded boy soprano. His incredible keyboard skills carried him successfully through the psychological and physiological rigors of mutation, which apparently occurred at the age of 15 or 16. His second wife, Anna Magdalena, is reputed to have been "a well-trained and accomplished singer" (Spitta). In his later years, escaping the depressing atmosphere of Leipzig in decline, Bach frequently visited an increasingly resplendent Dresden with his favorite son, Friedemann. There the most Italianized of German composers, Johann Hasse, and his wife Faustina, the most celebrated prima donna of her day, held forth at the opera. We are told that they greatly respected Bach and valued his friendship. Schweitzer tells us that Bach was present for the first performance, on 13 September 1731, of Hasse's opera, *Cleofide*, starring Faustina, and that they "more than once visited him in Leipzig," according to Forkel.

Obviously it is impossible to answer with any specificity, the question raised above. What Bach knew about Italian methods of teaching singing or how he was able to apply them can only be sought in his music or in the German commentaries published before, during and immediately after his life time. His own student Johann Friedrich Agricola wrote in 1757 a commentary and

German translation of the most significant work of the early eighteenth century, Tosi's *Observations on the Florid Song* (1723), as it is titled in Galliard's English translation of 1742. Agricola carried on the Bach tradition of organ playing, and, in 1772, Dr. Burney described him as "the best organ player in Berlin and the best singing master in Germany."

To understand what Bach could have known of the historical Italian school of singing, one should turn to Philip A. Duey's definitive study, *Bel Canto in its Golden Age: A Study of its Teaching Concepts* (1951, reprinted 1980). Duey gives generous space to the German sources, which uphold the Italian supremacy in vocal art. One might pay heed to the references and quotations pertaining to Agricola, Marpurg, Mattheson, Petri, Praetorius, Printz, Quantz and Scheibe.

Interestingly, Agricola, pupil of Bach, was also a pupil of Quantz, the great flute player. Quantz's *On Playing the Flute* appeared two years after Bach's death. In Edward R. Reilly's translation I find this to be an indispensable work for the Bach singer or player. Only five of the eighteen chapters are directed to the flute player. Let me urge the reader to ponder the short Chapter XI, "Of Good Execution in General in Singing and Playing." But my main concern in upholding Quantz is Chapter VII, "Of Taking Breath, in the Practice of the Flute." "Taking breath at the proper time is essential in playing wind instruments as well as in singing," writes Quantz. In his musical examples he indicates by a stroke above the note places "after which breath may be taken most conveniently." Quantz cautions: "it is self evident that you must take breath only when necessity requires, and not whenever notes like these occur."

Below you will find a Quantz-Reilly example which may be transposed—even an octave for bass and alto—and practiced easily and quietly. To which let me add the following: wind players and singers should avoid at all cost "snatching" or "catching" breath audibly and with any physical distortion of the player's or singer's body. Quiet execution is the mark of the master.

15

from *On Playing the Flute*, J.J. Quantz, 1752, tr. E. Reilly (see the Selected Reading List with this chapter for a complete citation).

Finally, relate Quantz's rules and suggestions to whatever you may read with regard to the art and technique of singing. What follows is my brief digest, as reflected in the current literature of pedagogy, of the Italian technique of *Appoggio*, or support in breathing and singing.

APPOGGIO
Traditional Italian Singing Technique

Defined as "a technique, associated with the historic Italian school, for establishing dynamic balance between the inspiratory, phonatory, and resonatory systems in singing." See Miller (1993), *Training Tenor Voices* (p.155).

Una nobile attitudine, the singer's noble posture (axial alignment) is described by V. Manfredini in his *Regole Armoniche*, 1797 See Duey, *Bel Canto* (1951)

<u>Breath Management</u>. In *Appoggio* (*appoggiare*-support), one differentiates the function of hypogastrium (lower abdomen) and epigastrium (upper abdomen). The diaphragm (inspiratory muscle) draws air into the lungs; it lowers somewhat to create the umbilical-epigastrial expansion at the midline. The singer maintains this expansion, thus creating the balance of power between inspiratory and expiratory muscles (lower abdominals) known in the Lamperti school as *la lotta vocale* (*lutte vocale*). This delicate balance greatly assists the singer in coordinating the breath to perform a variety of tasks (range, pitch, dynamics, *messa di voce*, etc.). Breathing for singing is well described by Mengozzi, who arrived in Paris in 1787, and became Professor of voice at the Paris Conservatory. See Timberlake, (1994,) "Apropos of Appoggio."

The term *Appoggio* constitutes a total system, encompassing sterno-costal-diaphragmatic-epigastric breathing. There is no hypogastric or lower distention here. Quiet breathing, muscular balance, ease of bearing and avoidance of pressure anywhere are characteristic of the technique.

Sing in the position of breathing—breathe in the position of singing. Posture is not altered in the course of renewing breath. The lungs must not be crowded and breathing is inaudible. The use of short onset exercises, while silently replenishing breath after each vowel or hum, is seen as key to elongating the breath cycle and maintaining the singer's equilibrium. Adages of *Appoggio* reinforce the importance of vital and inaudible exchanges: "the new breath is the release of the phonation." "The release is the new breath." "Sing on the gesture of inhalation." "Remain *ben appoggiata*."

Reporting on "Breathing Behavior During Singing," Sundberg reported that some singers activate the diaphragm only during inhalation and for reducing subglottal pressure at high lung volumes, while other singers have been found to co-contract it throughout the breath phrase (*The NATS Journal*, Jan/Feb 1993). Sundberg told me that he preferred a co-contracting to a flaccid diaphragm. That is my preference as well. I believe that the co-contraction of the diaphragm, steadily but not aggressively undertaken, may be reasonably considered an aspect of the traditional Italian technique of *Appoggio*. Practiced diligently, it might well produce better balanced singing and breathing in the performance of Bach's music.

Coloratura Exercises from selected choral works of J. S. Bach

Soprano

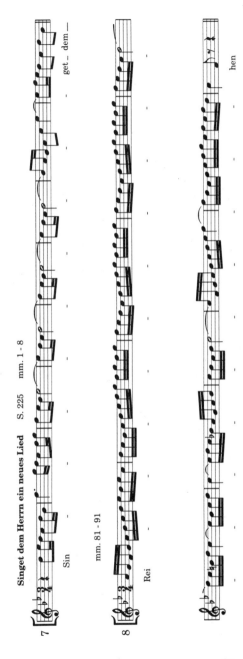

Singet dem Herrn ein neues Lied   S. 225   mm. 1 - 8

Sin ... get ... dem ...

mm. 81 - 91

Rei ... hen

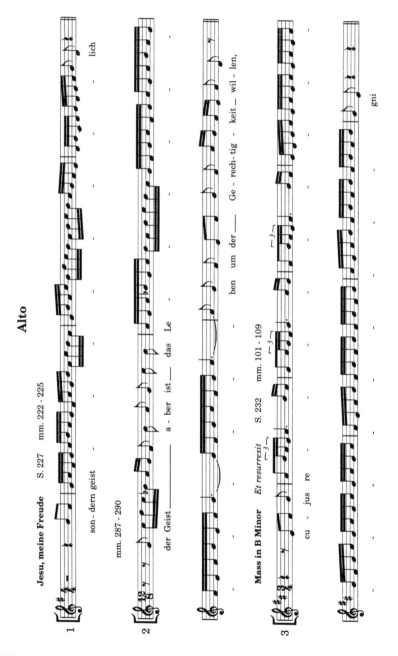

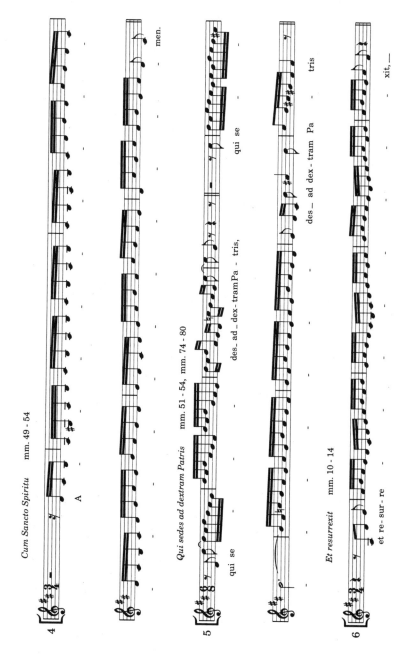

23

Tenor

Singet dem Herrn ein neues Lied   S. 225   mm. 109 - 118

mm. 2 - 8

mm. 13 - 20

Bass

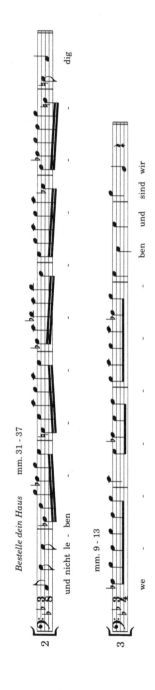

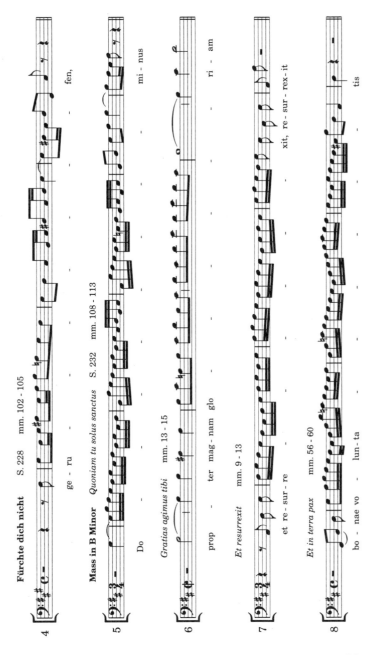

Selected Readings

VOICE

Duey, Philip A. *Bel Canto in its Golden Age: A Study of its Teaching Concepts*. New York: King's Crown Press, 1951, reprint Da Capo Press, 1980.

Gregg, Jean Westerman. "What Humming Can Do For You." *Journal of Singing*. Vol. 53, No. 5, 1996.

McKinney, James. *The Diagnosis and Correction of Vocal Faults, A manual for teachers of singing and for choir directors*. Nashville: Genevox Music Group, 1994.

Miller, Richard. *The Structure of Singing*. New York: Schirmer Books, 1986.

_____. *Training Tenor Voices*. New York: Schirmer Books, 1993.

Quantz, Johann Joachim (1752). *On Playing the Flute*. Tr. Edward R. Reilly. New York: The Free Press, 1966.

Sundberg, Johann. *The Science of the Singing Voice*. DeKalb, Illinois: Northern Illinois University Press, 1987.

_____. "Breathing Behavior During Singing." *The NATS Journal*. Vol. 50, No. 3, 1993.

Timberlake, Craig. "Pedagogical Perspectives, Past and Present: Laryngeal Positioning." *The NATS Journal*. Vol. 51, No. 1, 1994.

_____. "Pedagogical Perspectives, Past and Present: Apropos of Appoggio." *The NATS Journal*. Vol. 51, No. 2, 1994.

_____. "Pedagogical Perspectives, Past and Present: Apropos of Appoggio, II." *The NATS Journal*. Vol. 51, No. 3, 1994.

INTERNATIONAL PHONETIC ALPHABET

Betteridge, Rev. Harold T. *Cassell's German/English, English/German Dictionary*. New York: MacMillan, 1978.

Cartier and Todaro. *The Phonetic Alphabet*. Dubuque, IA: Wm. C. Brown, 1983.

Kenyon, John and Knott, Thomas. *A Pronouncing Dictionary of American English*. Springfield, Mass.: Merriam–Webster, 1953.

Marshall, Madeleine. *The Singer's Manual of English Diction*. New York: G. Schirmer, 1953.

Odom, William. *German for Singers*. New York: Schirmer Books, 1981.

Siebs, Theodor. *Deutsche Bühnenaussprache – Hochsprache*. Berlin: Gruyter, 1958.

Wall, Joan. *International Phonetic Alphabet for Singers*. Dallas: Pst . . . Inc., 1989.

Wall, et. al. *Diction for Singers: A concise reference for English, Italian, Latin, German, French and Spanish Pronunciation*. Dallas: Pst . . . Inc., 1990.

MISCELLANEOUS

Castel, Nico and Graham, Arthur. "Pedagogical Opinion: German Diction—A Dialogue." *Journal of Singing*. Vol. 53, No. 3, 1996.

"Healthy Vocal Technique and the Performance of Early Music." A Pronouncement of The American Academy of Teachers of Singing. *The NATS Journal*. Vol. 51, No. 2, 1994.

Marshall, Robert L. "Bach the Progressive: Observations on his Later Works." *The Music of Johann Sebastian Bach*. New York: Schirmer Books, 1989.

Munro, Marth and Larson, Maren. "The Influence of Body Integration on Voice Production." *Journal of Singing*. Vol. 52, No. 2, 1996.

Neumann, Frederick. "Authenticity and Vocal Vibrato." *New Essays in Performance Practice*. Ann Arbor, MI: UMI Research, 1989.

Sataloff, Robert T. and Titze, Ingo. *Vocal Health and Science*. Jacksonville, FL.: National Association of Teachers of Singing, 1991.

Titze, Ingo. "Lip and Tongue Trills—What do they do for us?" *Journal of Singing*. Vol. 53, No. 3, 1996.

_____. "More on Messa di Voce." *Journal of Singing*. March/April, 1996.

Vowels

IPA Symbol	English	German	Italian	French
[i]	we, sea	Zion sieh, wie	mi, tradi	oui, gris
[ɪ]	give, sieve	ist nichts ich, singet		
[e]	chaos, weight	Seele, Ehre	pena, venti (twenty)	été, quai
[ɛ]	when, said	wenn, Herr	tempo, venti (winds)	être, père esprit
[æ]	at, band, apple			
[a]	valor, talon	alles, kalt		égal, rare
[ɑ]	father, God, psalm	Vater, Namen	padre, grande	âme, orage calme
[ɔ]	awe, call, sought	Sonne, Gott	morte, core sotto, sopra	porte, cor votre
[o]	robe, grove, cope	Rose, loben Sohn, ohne	amore, non	haut, flot, beau
[ʊ]	book, should	Huld, junge stumm, Mutter		
[u]	soon, tune, through	Mut, Ruhe, Fuss	un, più, su	trouver, ou vous, sou
[ʌ]	up, love, son, cuff, nation			

IPA Symbol	English	German	Italian	French
[ə] (schwa)	above, parade	heilige, Gemeine		le, je, [œ] regard
[y]		über, glühen, Füsse		lune, tu, surprise
[Y]		Glück, Küsse		
[ø]	learn, tern	schön, Töne		peu, voeux, mieux
[œ]		köpfe		heure

Semi-Vowels (Glides) and Diphthongs

IPA Symbol	English	German	Italian	French
[j]	young, meow yes, you	ja, jugend	più, pieno	hier, pied, papier
[w]	wish		uomo, Guido	moi, droit, loi
[aɪ]	Christ, prize	[ae] Mai, seine	[ai] mai	
[aʊ]	house, cowl	[ao] Haus, braun	[au] aura	
[ei]	way, weigh		[ei] Lei [ɔi] vuoi	
[ɔɪ]	boy, rejoice	[ɔø] Freude, Kreuz		

IPA Symbols - Consonant Sounds

IPA Symbol	Voiceless	Articulation	IPA	Voiced
[p]	Paul	bilabial	[b]	Bob
[t]	tone	lingua-alveolar	[d]	drone
[k]	cane	velar	[g]	gain
[f]	fat	labiodental	[v]	vat
[θ]	things	linguadental	[ð]	these
[s]	decease	dental	[z]	disease
[ʃ]	sh! mission	lingua-alveolar	[ʒ]	vision
[ç]	ich (German)	palatal		
[x]	ach (German)	velar		
[h]	ha - ha! (aspirate)	glottal	[?] (stroke of glottis)	uh-oh!
[tʃ]	church	lingua-alveolar	[dʒ]	George
[ts]	cats	lingua-dental	[dz]	cads

Nasal Consonants

[m]	mama	bilabial nasal
[n]	nanny	lingua-alveolar nasal
[ŋ]	song	velar nasal
[ɲ]	onion (Eng)	gnocchi, lasagna (It)

Other voiced consonants

[ʎ]	foglia, moglie (Italian)
[l]	lull, lily, Liebe, fleur de lis, etc.
[ɻ]	rare (retroflex r)
[r̃]	rolled r

The Lutheran Chorale:
A Key to the
Interpretation of Bach's Choral Music

Dr. James E. Jordan, Jr.

The preparation and performance of any choral work by J.S. Bach necessitates the study and understanding of Bach's dramatic use of the German Lutheran chorale. Noted Bach scholar Alfred Mann states that:

> The chorale stands at the center of Bach's work. Ranging from the small organ preludes in the early *Orgelbüchlein* and the stark four-part settings that conclude many of the cantatas to the immense chorale fantasy that opens *St. Matthew Passion*, the use of the chorale is the key to Bach's oeuvre. The chorale determines the work of the Leipzig cantor as does no other musical form.[1]

The chorale is also important to understand because of its personal significance to the people of Bach's time. Bach and his fellow countrymen knew German Lutheran chorales as people today might know "Amazing Grace" or "O Come, all ye Faithful." The chorales were more than simply familiar—they were the music of the people and were important for learning and teaching the rudiments of the Christian faith. Albert Schweitzer, in speaking of the origins of the chorale tunes, notes:

> It was . . . natural to impress existing melodies into the service of the Church, sacred melodies at first, and then, when these did not suffice, secular ones . . . . That the

object was conversion . . . is shown by the title of a col-
lection that appeared in Frankfurt in 1571: Street Songs,
cavalier songs, mountain songs, transformed into
Christian and moral songs, for the abolishing in course of
time of the bad and vexatious practice of singing idle and
shameful songs in the streets, in fields, and at home, by
substituting for them good, sacred, honest words . . . .[2]

Thus, gaining textual and musical knowledge of the chorales
is indispensable for the modern choir to re-interpret music that
Bach aimed toward the parishioners of his day. As this brief discussion has been primarily generated from study of the *St.
Matthew Passion*, dramatic and musical points of reference are
taken from this work.

In the *St. Matthew Passion*, Bach often uses the strict four-
part chorales to give pause in the re-enacted drama for reflection
by the congregation. This makes the study of a literal translation
an excellent starting point for analysis for four reasons:

1. Knowing the textual point of a phrase (i.e. , subject, verb,
adjectives, etc. . . .) allows the singer a better "feel" for the language to express the essence of the text. Just as the solo singer
studies the literal and prosaic translations of a text, the choral
singer also needs this study to personalize the work.

2. Giving several choices for the translation of a single word
(or simply an occasional difference from the "norm") helps open
a broader "picture" of a given word or phrase. Also, in the
appropriate moments, a general discussion of certain words or
phrases will help performers to "own" the text for themselves.

3. A knowledge of the original text enables the choir to gain
a genuine understanding of the vision Bach communicates
through his juxtaposition of text and music.

4. Because much of the music of the Baroque and especially
that of Bach springs forth from an emotion or feeling implied or

understood within the actual text. A quote from *The Bach Reader* puts this succinctly:

> In the opinion of Bach's time, one of the foremost aims of music, sacred or secular, was the *Ausdrückung der Affecten*, the expression of the *affetti* (mood, emotion, or passion) . . . . Bach himself strove sedulously to vest his texts with the most intense, appropriate music . . . . He carefully suited his music to the mood and meaning of the text even in his organ chorales, where the text itself was not presented with the music, though it was familiar to the congregation. He expected his pupils to do the same . . . . (one in particular stated) he had been instructed by the Capellmeister Bach to present chorales "not just offhand but in accordance with the *Affekt* of the words."[3]

It is after gaining this textual insight that the next step of interpretation can be taken: musical analysis as it relates to the text. In this context, the study of musical form and subtleties guides one toward a greater expression of the text. A primary musical analysis could be as simple as noting that in the first three settings of the famous "Passion Chorale," there are no harmonic differences save the lowering of the key setting, each time by a half-step. Thus, the essence of the text takes on even more significance as the singers realize that the pitches move lower with each repetition. Analysis of this type is quick, convincing and intriguing as it gives access to musical elements that have direct textual correlations.

The next logical step could be a brief analysis of the final setting of the "Passion Chorale" which contains harmonic variations from the other versions. With knowledge of text and the harmonic relationship of the first three settings, a more detailed analysis of the final setting to find points of greatest harmonic interest clarifies the vision of the text, as particular words stand out in relief through harmonic variation. One example is found in mm 9-10 of "Wenn ich einmal soll scheiden." The three lower voices change from diatonic to chromatic motion over the text

"Wenn mir am allerbängsten wird" ("When I become over-whelmingly afraid"), intensifying the text. This type of text painting is found throughout Bach's choral works making the chorale an excellent vehicle for study of Bach's own use of *Affekt*.

Next, a choir could study Bach's formal idea of repeating the "Passion Chorale" in the *St. Matthew Passion* as another level of musical and dramatic unity. This creates both musical and dramatic links through various sections of the work. Again, he capitalizes on what was already familiar to the people to create a form to which they could readily respond. This "interweaving" of chorales throughout the work also united the traditions of chanting the Passion texts and singing chorales on Good Friday. One of the most poignant examples of this "interweaving" occurs following the chorus in which Jesus' disciples ask him concerning his betrayal: "Herr, bin ichs?" ("Lord, is it I?"). The chorale immediately following opens "Ich bins, ich sollte büßen" ("It is I who should atone"). Similarly, a dramatic link is heard between the recitative in which Jesus tells his disciples they will flee from him and the opening text of the ensuing chorale "Ich will hier bei dir stehen; verachte mich doch nicht." ("I will stand by you here—please do not scorn me!").

Finally, the choir could then study Bach's use of the chorales as cantus firmi. For example, the opening chorus of the *St. Matthew Passion* is in the style of the French *Tombeau* (funeral march). The chorale, *O Lamm Gottes unschuldig*, (the German "Agnus Dei") marked *soprano in ripieno*, enters over the double choruses placing the focus, through both sound and structure, upon Jesus as the Lamb of God. By bringing the unadorned chorale within the opening chorus, Bach sets the precedent in this work for using the chorale as a major thematic device.[4] The final movement of Part I, *O Mensch bewein dein Sünde gross (O Man, bewail thy great sin)*, is also a large chorale fantasia in which the phrases of the chorale actually determine the structure of the entire piece.

Although this chapter gives only a brief overview, the choir which takes an approach similar to this, joining an initial textual understanding with an ensuing musical analysis, will find that through a natural growth from text to music, Bach opens a "personal door" to expressing the text through his music. Even though the examples cited in this chapter are specific to a given work, Bach's use of the chorale is predominant in his entire *œuvre*. Given that he once stated that "Where there is a reverent performance of music, God is ever-present in his mercy," it makes perfect sense that it would be the chorale—the choral voice of the Reformed Lutheran Church—that would serve as the inroad to a better understanding of his choral music.

Notes:

1. "Chorale Cantatas" from *Bethlehem Bach Studies*, Mann, Alfred, The American Choral Foundation, Bethlehem, Pennsylvania, 1985, p. 26.
2. From Albert Schweitzer's *J.S. Bach* as quoted in: *Bach's Chorales*, Charles Sanford Terry, Cambridge University Press, 1915, pp. x-xiii.
3. *The Bach Reader*, David, Hans T. and Mendel, Arthur, W.W. Norton and Company, Inc., New York, 1966, pp. 33-34.
4. This tune was probably first done as an organ solo, to which Bach added a text in later performances.

"Soli Deo Gloria"

Fr. Martin Shannon

Only when music combines with faith,
and beauty with truth, does it receive the
full authority to serve in the sanctuary.

—O. Söhngen, *"Theologische Grundlagen der Kirchenmusik"*

Johann Sebastian Bach. The very name conjures up a profusion of images and emotions, each peculiar to the individual who is either hearing or performing one of the composer's many masterpieces—the director who endeavors to understand and decide upon implied tempos or varied interpretations; the young organ student who spends hours rehearsing the same page of fuguing eighth-note runs; the choral singer striving to perfect both the German as well as the musical phrasing of Bach's intricately woven patterns; the soloist, instrumental or vocal, who labors to keep a pure intonation even as the range and rhythm seem to propel one on a musical journey that has a life all its own; and, of course, the listener who, perhaps unaware of the intricate and intense difficulties involved, sits as if under a spell and wonders how such beautiful music could be performed so well, much less how it was thought of in the first place.

But even these images are incomplete, for they focus primarily on the technical prowess of this musical genius. Is that enough of an explanation, however, for the effective combination of beauty and truth in J.S. Bach's music which has made his work such an enduring element in the worship of Christ's Church? By itself, does the compilation of notes make a piece of music "beautiful" or "truthful"? Is it only a matter of getting one's arithmetic right—making all of the "numbers" add up correctly—that instills a piece of music with that element of grace which stirs the human heart and inspires the soul to hope or to gratitude, to wonder or to sorrow?

It is not the purpose of this brief chapter to debate the many philosophies of music as a bearer of beauty and truth. We accept that it does. But, behind the medium stands the artist, the flesh and blood person, whose own passions and insights are somehow added to the recipe, so that what is "created" is more than the sum of the tangible ingredients. Robert Frost, for example, conveyed his love for nature, as well as his skill with language, under the guise of words and phrases. Claude Monet displayed his fascination with sun and light, as well as his talent with the brush, in the form of color and image. And Johann Sebastian Bach expressed his faith and his dedication to God's glory, as well as his mastery of musical concepts, in patterns of sound and harmony. "For Bach," wrote Robin A. Leaver, "the ascription *S.D.G.* (Soli Deo Gloria—"To God alone the glory") at the end of his manuscripts was no empty formality; it was an aim he pursued throughout his life."[1] Bach the Christian, Bach the believer. To appreciate more fully the character of his music requires that we more fully appreciate the character of his faith.

Bach was born into a devout Lutheran family. This is of utmost importance. As a boy, he attended the old Latin school of St. George in Eisenach, Germany from which Luther himself had graduated some 200 years earlier. The region of Bach's upbringing and of his later service to the church was, as described by one author, "permeated by the legacy of Martin Luther, with his radical emphasis on a living, personal, Bible-based Christianity. Luther himself had been a musician, declaring music to be second only to the word of God itself. Bach was to be the Reformer's greatest musical disciple."[2] The roots of orthodox Lutheranism grew deep in the Bach household and became "the central presupposition of [Bach's] thinking and acting."[3] This was no mere allegiance to what would eventually become, like so many other theological persuasions, a dry formulation of doctrinal statements or academic exercises. It is clear from at least one of Bach's letters that his faith was of personal proportion. Writing to the landlord of his recalcitrant son, he reveals the kind of faith which at times can be the only solace for the heart of a distressed father:

> What shall I say or do further? Since no admonition, nor even any living care and *assistance* will suffice any more, I must bear my cross in patience, and leave my unruly son to God's Mercy alone, doubting not that He will hear my sorrowful pleading, and in the end will so work upon him, according to His Holy Will, that he will learn to acknowledge that the lesson is owing wholly and alone to Divine Goodness.[4]

One author has suggested that from the pens of his friends or family members, "nothing of the true inner Bach has come down to us."[5] Yet, even setting aside the resounding testimony of his own music, such words as those above are ample witness to the "inner Bach" and to the quality of his faith and the depth of his own trust in a loving and merciful God. When extended to influence the character not only of his prayers, but of his musical compositions, this faith may be compared to the breath which animates the fleshly form and without which that form is lifeless. As one of his many historians has asked, "In view of Bach's course of life, can one even seriously consider it possible that Bach could create and work in his liturgical office and assignment without any inner personal tie to the liturgy and without any binding relation to the interests of the Gospel?"[6]

In the more than twenty-five years during which he served in Leipzig, as Cantor of the Thomasschule (1723-1750) and as guest Capellmeister to the court of Frederick August II of Poland and Lithuania (1736-1750), Bach wrote extensively for the church. Such music was an integral part of the divine service, and served to further the overarching purpose to which he had dedicated his work so many years before. In a letter requesting that he be dismissed from the post of organist of the Blasiuskirche

(Mühlhausen) in 1708, Bach clearly identified his aim in life to compose and direct *regulirte kirchen musik zu Gottes Ehren*— "well-regulated church music to the glory of God."[7]

Toward the accomplishment of that end he embraced the tenets of orthodox Lutheranism, resisting the inroads of both Calvinism and Pietism. Though he considered music to be a gift from God, Calvin saw it as belonging only in the worldly domain. He considered instrumental music to be "senseless and absurd" and, as over against the use of any harmonies, permitted only the unison singing of the Psalms in worship. This was the legacy which he left to his followers. No such hard and fast distinction was made by Bach between sacred and secular music. Gerhard Herz writes: "Doubts as to whether his music was sacred or not existed for [Bach] as little as they did for Luther and his church. For both of them there existed only one music which became sacred or profane through the spirit in which it was performed."[8] One can imagine Bach saying it in much the same way as did Luther himself:

> Next to the word of God, music deserves the highest praise. . . . I am not of the opinion that all arts are to be cast down and destroyed on account of the gospel, as some fanatics protest; on the other hand, I would gladly see all arts, especially music, in the service of him who has given and created them.

Music, then, may be seen not only as a thoroughly *appropriate* vehicle but as an *excellent* vehicle for conveying the truth of the Gospel. For example, describing Bach's setting of the Nicene Creed in his *Mass in B Minor*, Albert Schweitzer sees Bach "the theologian" at work, intricately weaving together the echoing and reechoing voices as they proclaim, "*Deum de Deo, lumen de lumine, Deum verum de Deo vero,* [God *of* God, light *of* light, true God *of* true God]." It is of interest to note that Schweitzer himself displayed a good deal of animosity toward the orthodox doctrines of the Trinity and the person of Christ. That animosity was more than challenged, however, not by scholastic treatises on the Trinity, but by Bach's musical setting, and Schweitzer was compelled to acknowledge:

> To the dogmatist Bach the parallel passages [regarding the mystery of Christ's identity with both God and man] . . . were not merely empty sounds to be turned into music; he knew what the formulae meant, and translated them into terms of music. He makes both singers sing the same notes, but in such a way that it does not amount to the same thing; the voices follow each other in strict canonic imitation; the one proceeds out of the other just as Christ proceeds out of God. . . . Bach thus proves that the dogma can be expressed much more clearly and satisfactorily in music than in verbal formulae.[9]

So much for Bach's answer to Calvinism. As for the teachings of the eighteenth century Pietist movement, Bach may be seen as firmly resisting the ardent individualism and escapism which it advocated, while at the same time borrowing from its emphasis on subjective faith and moral earnestness. The place of music in the worship of the church was not primarily for the purpose of personal edification, but for the glorification of God. Bach's compositions clearly find their places within the liturgical framework of the church's corporate worship. Nevertheless, unless the church's music could incite its listeners to an ever deepening devotion to God, it did nothing more than entertain.

Following these lines, historian Jaroslav Pelikan sees Bach as maintaining the delicate balance of two potentially competing emphases—Christ as Lord (*Herr*) of the church, and Christ as Savior (*Heiland*) of the individual soul. The subtle shift in emphasis from the objective Christ *for* us (the "Lamb of God") to the subjective Christ *in* us (the "Bridegroom of the Church"), represented by Pietist spirituality, is resisted by Bach, in favor of maintaining both in a necessary tension. One can certainly see both in such works as the *St. Matthew Passion*, sometimes juxtaposed within the same line. As Pelikan points out:

The accident of language by which, in German, "Seelenbräutigam" rhymed with "Gottes Lamm" made that a couplet which would appear not only in the Drese-Zinzendorf song that Bach set as BWV 409 but almost literally countless times within Bach's own lifework . . . for example, in the opening double chorus of the Saint Matthew Passion.[10]

There, Bach summons his listeners: "Sehet den Bräutigam, seht ihn als wie ein Lamm, sehet." ("See the Bridegroom, see Him, like a Lamb is He, see.") The Christ who is portrayed in this musical narrative is both *Herr und Heiland.*

There is yet one more crucial piece of evidence witnessing to the significant role of Bach's faith in his compositions. Robin A. Leaver has compiled and edited a volume of glosses from the Calov Bible Commentary which was studied by Bach, and in which the composer made a number of marginal notes. Upon Bach's death, more than eighty books were found in his library, all of spiritual nature, including the complete works of Luther and numerous writings by Luther's followers. Exactly how the Calov Commentary was discovered later in the twentieth century makes for some fascinating reading, but for the purposes of this chapter, it is the notes made by Bach which are of primary interest. Three may be cited.

The first is made next to a passage from 1 Chronicles 25, which describes the establishment of both choral and instrumental worship for the assembled people of God under King David. Bach underlines Calov's accompanying comment that the musicians are to "express the Word of God in spiritual songs and psalms, sing them in the temple and at the same time to play instruments." And in the margin he himself comments, "This chapter is the true foundation of all God-pleasing church music." We hear the echo once again of his call for "a well-regulated church music to the glory of God."

The second comment appears in the margin opposite 1 Chronicles 28:21 in which is described the divisions of the priests and the Levites "for all the service of the house of God." It is already noted that musicians were among the Levites, and so Bach observes, "Splendid proof that, besides other arrangements of the service of worship, music too was instituted by the Spirit of God through David." Leaver elucidates:

> Here Bach goes further than his marginal note on 1 Chronicles 25 and explicitly states that music in the liturgy is a Spirit-given institution. It needs to be remembered that the musicians of the old covenant were a division of the Levites and were thus "ordained" to their office. Thus music, and those who perform it, are not to be regarded as optional extras that can easily be dispensed with; they are essentials in the worship of the people of God.[11]

Finally, Bach observes next to 2 Chronicles 5:13, which describes the house of the Lord being filled with a heavenly cloud when the music has ended, "Where there is devotional music, God with his grace is always present." In this comment, says Leaver, "Bach has beautifully summed up the conviction that through appropriate music in the service of worship the worshipers become aware of the presence and grace of God."[12]

It may be observed from the above discussion, and specifically from hand-written notations in the Calov Commentary, that for Johann Sebastian Bach, the primary principle which sustains the role of music in the church is not so much theological as it is doxological. The implication, of course, is truly theological in the best sense of the word. Such music conveys a "word about God." Most especially, that word, in Bach's view, was to be a word of praise *to the glory of God*. This, above all else, summarizes his passion as well as his message. And it is the essential ingredient which binds all the notes and rhythms, all the texts and hymns, all the numerology and symbolism into a cohesive whole, and without which they would be left as so much leavenless dough. "The aim and final reason [of all music]," he said to his students, "should be none else but the glory of God and the recreation of the human mind. Where this is not observed, there will be no real music but only a devilish hubbub."[13]

Notes:

1. Robin A. Leaver, *J.S. Bach and Scripture: Glosses from the Calov Bible Commentary*, (St Louis: Concordia, 1985) 107.
2. Patrick Kavanaugh, *The Spiritual Lives of Great Composers*, (Nashville: Sparrow Press, 1992) 13.
3. Günther Stiller, *Johann Sebastian Bach and Liturgical Life in Leipzig*, (St. Louis: Concordia, 1984) 210.
4. Hans T. David and Arthur Mendel, eds., *The Bach Reader: A Life of Johann Sebastian Bach in Letters and Documents*, rev. ed., (New York: W.W. Norton & Company, 1966) 160.
5. Gerhard Herz, *Essays on J.S. Bach*, (Ann Arbor: UMI Research Press, 1985) 7.
6. Stiller, 200.
7. *The Bach Reader*, 60.
8. Herz, 2.
9. Albert Schweitzer, *J.S. Bach*, 2 vols., trans. Ernest Newman, (New York: Macmillan, 1966) 2:318-19.
10. Jaroslav Pelikan, *Bach Among the Theologians*, (Philadelphia: Fortress Press, 1986) 65.
11. Leaver, 95-6.
12. Ibid., 97.
13. *The Bach Reader*, 32-3.

Ornamentation

Dr. John Butt

Ornamentation normally refers to two related fields. The most common usage concerns the specific symbols a composer such as Bach employs to indicate an ornamental formula (e.g. trill, turn); it also relates to the concept of free embellishment (sometimes termed "diminutions" or "passages") that might be improvised by the performer or indicated didactically (or as a suggestion) by the composer.

The very term "ornamentation" and the French and German equivalents current in Bach's time ("Agréments" and "Manieren") may suggest that the issue is one of only secondary, cosmetic importance. Frederick Neumann, in by far the most informed and intellectually challenging study of Bach's ornamentation (1978), insists that performers be alerted to the dichotomy of the structural and the ornamental in music, in other words to be aware of the relative importance of each note to its neighbor. While he acknowledges that there can often be a merging of the categories "structure" and "ornament"—a fluid interplay between the two—he insists that the performer internalize the notion that the structure implies weight and importance, while ornament suggests lightness and easy flow.

Yet the intensity of Neumann's writing and the remarkable degree of bigotry that the subject of ornamentation (particularly Bach's) seems to evince, often gives the impression that there is no subject of greater importance to the satisfactory performance of Bach. Moreover, there is evidence that certain composer-performers of Bach's age were equally didactic: Couperin's injunction that players should neither add nor take away from what he has indicated in the notation (*Troisième Livre*, 1722) is well known, and C.P.E. Bach's proscriptions (1753; no pre-beat appoggiaturas, no main-note trills beginning on the beat) are perhaps better known than his many perceptive suggestions. Finally, we have J.A. Scheibe's criticism (1737) of Bach himself; the assertion that Bach indicated every little note—normally the prerogative of the performer—in the notation itself (Bach Dokumente, II, p. 286-7).

Scheibe is almost certainly referring to the wider area of improvised embellishment here, not to the narrower sense of the ornaments as indicated by specific symbols (mostly of French origin). In a certain sense, Bach's notated music is suffused with ornamentation; if one were to apply Neumann's conceptual dichotomy of structure and ornament, it is often difficult to distinguish the two—one ornament can be "structural" in relation to another and if one succeeds in finding something "structural" (and such a notion is often rather more subjective that many "objective" analysts would like to admit) it is not necessarily of particular musical interest. In short, the very subtlety of Bach's music may lie in the notion that everything can be ornamental and structural simultaneously; the ornamented texture *is* the music and thus as essential as anything one can hope to find. Furthermore, even in Neumann's sense, the ornamental is not necessarily lighter than that which it elaborates. After all, the most basic function of musical ornament, the controlled and expressive use of dissonance, draws attention to itself and, as with a figure of speech, cuts across the grain of the "dull" norm.

Marpurg, writing somewhat after Bach's death, refers to the above sense of ornamentation (i.e., diminution, whether notated by the composer or improvised by the performer) as the "willkür-lich" (optional) ornamentation. The more usual use of the term "ornamentation" today refers to Marpurg's "wesentlich" (essential) ornaments, those indicated by specific symbols, or added analogously by the performer. Clearly there is some interplay between the two categories—the appoggiatura (or *accentus* in German terminology) as a one-note grace is both the simplest level of diminution and the simplest ornament indicated by a symbol—but generally the symbol will refer to something that cannot exactly (or even consistently) be indicated in regular notation.

Two pieces of evidence are most often cited as the guide of Bach's ornament symbols: the "Explication" which Bach wrote at the outset of the *Clavier-Büchlein* for the nine-year-old Wilhelm Friedemann Bach (1720) and the chapter on ornamentation from the keyboard treatise of Bach's second son, Carl Philipp Emanuel (1753), who repeatedly records his indebtedness to his father's methods. Several other tables of ornaments are sometimes noted: those found in the Möller manuscript and the Andreas-Bach-Buch (the earliest significant Bach sources, compiled by Bach's older brother, Johann Christoph) and the copy of D'Anglebert's comprehensive table that Bach himself included in his copy of organ and harpsichord music by DeGrigny and Dieupart. Neither of Christoph's manuscripts was copied while Bach was actually a pupil of his brother; the three tables rather imply that the Bach circle became acquainted with the French system of ornament symbols during the period spanning Bach's Arnstadt and Weimar years (the fact that Bach included the table at the end of his De Grigny copy might suggest that he still needed it c.1709-12).

Bach's "Explication" apparently derives from D'Anglebert's system and its principles seem to accord with those later offered by C.P.E. Bach—all trills begin on the upper note and may or may not conclude with a suffix; appoggiaturas begin on the beat and normally take up half the length of the main note. However, many writers have noted that the "Explication" provides only the most rudimentary guide to ornaments and that the realization of such ornaments in practice will require an approach far more flexible than whatever can be indicated in notation. Frederick Neumann and, more recently, Paul Badura-Skoda (1990,1993), have argued at length that Bach took a flexible (though not, apparently, liberal) approach to ornamentation, allowing main-note trills and pre-beat appoggiaturas, and that the player should take a wide range of factors—such as dissonance treatment, voice-leading and melodic line—into account when deciding how to interpret an ornament. Two of the opinions that Neumann expresses throughout his writing are among the most valuable within the entire field of historical performance—that there was never a uniformity of practice spanning many decades and locations, and that treatises and tables need to be used with caution, taking into account who designed them for whom and at what time. As he stresses, with regard to the "Explication", "the table tells us that the graces in question *may* have the shapes indicated, but not that they *must* have these shapes which, as will be shown, are often disqualified by musical evidence" (p.127).

Neumann is right to draw attention to the fact that the evidence from German theoretical and notational sources of the late seventeenth century shows a wide range of applications for the one-note grace (*accentus*) and that the onbeat Vorschlag is a French import, evident, for instance, in Walther's *Lexicon* of 1732 (but clearly not as a replacement for all the other applications). Another figure close to Bach is his predecessor in Leipzig, Johann Kuhnau, who coined the concept of the *Clavier Übung* with his two publications of 1689 and 1692. Not only does the notation of these publications show a wide range of *accentus* ornaments, indicated by dashes, many of which can be interpreted as nothing other than the pre-beat *Nachschlag*, but the dashes are extremely profuse, far more than the norm for Bach's notated appoggiaturas (something which Neumann does not readily acknowledge). Kuhnau's notation, incidentally, has something in common with English keyboard sources of the seventeenth century where the dashes imply a performance highly nuanced by graces, almost indiscriminately at times, it seems. In Kuhnau's later two publications these are not indicated, since Kuhnau assumes the performer to have assimilated the practice and to be able to use his own judgment. Clearly he sees the ornaments as belonging to the performer's style and his notated suggestions do not seem to be the issue of profound thought. It is likely that Bach was brought up in this tradition of free, performer-oriented ornamentation, however much his practice later developed.

The German tradition shows that the nearly standard main-note trill of the seventeenth century is still viable well into the next century and that the influence of the French upper-note trill came at a comparatively late stage (c. 1696, according to Neumann). Furthermore, most seventeenth-century sources of keyboard music with written-out trills (following the Frescobaldi-Froberger tradition) show them beginning on the main note, so, Badura-Skoda moreover affirms that the simple *Pralltriller* (first described by C.P.E. Bach), the short trill with a single oscillation (i.e., the inversion of the mordant) should often be applied to Bach's music even if it is not specified in sources of his time.

Much of the justification Neumann and Badura-Skoda offer with regard to their revolution against the orthodoxy of performance practice is based on apparent problems of voice-leading, particularly parallel octaves and fifths. Peter Williams (1984) (see Annotated Bibliography, p. 61) takes a refreshingly liberal approach to all these issues (noting that ornamentation is a subject that attracts a certain kind of "evangelistic pedantry," p. 225), and asserts that consecutives are simply not a major consideration when it comes to ornamentation, since the ear seldom detects them unaided by the eye. Certainly, a similar opinion is expressed by Bach's own cousin J.G. Walther in his 'Praecepta' of 1708, who quotes J.G. Ahle's assertion that an ornament can neither cause a compositional lapse nor mitigate one. Thus, although Neumann and Badura-Skoda may well be right in claiming there was more variability in ornament practice than modern orthodoxy affirms, their motives might rather be their own personal preference that every element of ornamentation be subject to all the laws of harmony. Moreover, neither seems prepared to countenance that Bach may have been brought up to ornament profusely, if not somewhat indiscriminately.

David Schulenberg (*The Keyboard Music of J.S. Bach*, New York, 1992) sees Bach's attitude towards ornamentation as progressively hardening, so that in the course of many years of teaching "what were originally offered as suggestions might have gradually become prescriptions" (p. 132). Thus Emanuel's treatise may be seen as the end of a process that Bach began with the ornaments table of 1720. Neumann might then exaggerate when he paints Emanuel as the "villain" who led us astray, since the hardening attitude seems already to have begun in France, to have become prevalent in Germany during the 1730s and 40s, and to have been fostered by Bach himself. However, Neumann's assertion that the Berlin school, of which Emanuel was a part, was acting under the influence of Prussian militarism the "categorical imperative of ornamental ethics" (p. 39) is a challenging thought, one that could also be directed to the absolutism of the French court. Moreover, Bach seems to have progressively aligned himself with the royalty of the Saxon court, and towards the end of his life, the Prussian court, suggesting that he was part of the growing absolutist tide. He does indeed seem to have become increasingly prescriptive, frequently adding ornaments to the instrumental and vocal parts of his cantatas, and he evidently took great care in preparing the *Clavier Übung* engravings, giving particular attention to the correction of ornaments in his personal copies.

Several questions seem to come to the fore here: Was Bach as didactic as a performer as he attempted to be on paper and as a teacher? Should we try and mimic the apparent progression from liberal ornamentation to controlled, "hardened" categories according to the period from which any particular piece comes. If we were sure we knew them, should Bach's ornamental habits be unquestioningly followed in any case?

The behavior of ornament pedants today, and the evidence of many writers of the time (who both lay down prescriptions on paper and also emphasize that the correct style can only be attained through the imitation of good performers), perhaps reveal the nearest we get to a fundamental truth regarding ornamentation. It is a question of style, identifying with a particular fashion. Thus something seemingly insignificant in one environment becomes a social *gaffe* in another; to play a wrong ornament at court is as bad as wearing the wrong dress at court. The ornamental indeed becomes "structural" (i.e., of paramount importance), the uniformity against which Neumann railed was not so much the historical style that its proponents supposed as a matter of class identity within performance of the late twentieth century, an identity that has (from even before Neumann's death in 1995) become more diverse and open to change.

For a comprehensive table of all the symbols Bach employs, see Klotz p. 26ff and Badura-Skoda p. 307ff.

References

C.P.E. Bach, *Essay on the True Art of Playing Keyboard Instruments*, Vol. 1 (1753), tr. W.J. Mitchell (London, 1949).

P. Badura-Skoda, *Interpreting Bach at the Keyboard* (1990), tr. A. Clayton (Oxford, 1993).

H. Klotz, *Die Ornamentik der Klavier und Orgelwerke von J. S. Bach* (Kassel, 1984).

F. Neumann, *Ornamentation in Baroque and Post-Baroque Music* (Princeton, 1978).

This essay is taken from *The Oxford Companion to Bach*, ed. Malcolm Boyd (Oxford University Press, 1998) and is used by permission.

Thoughts on English Translations in Bach's Vocal Works

Dr. David H. Chalmers

The cantatas of Bach are some of the richest repertoire available to the church musician and choir to express the truths of the Christian faith. Communicating the depth of meaning in these pieces is a priority, and yet the German language may be a stumbling block for many. Does one spend the time to learn the language phonetically, or is a singing translation a real possibility in these works? This author explored some possibilities to see where the pitfalls are and also where there might be some real help in finding translations.

Perhaps the best known personality in this area is the music scholar Henry Drinker. Drinker was a lawyer by profession but devoted himself to music as a serious interest. In his study of vocal music, he was concerned that the words should be understood but also fit the music. Between 1941 and 1954 he translated the texts of nearly all of Bach's vocal works as well as numerous songs by nineteenth century composers. These translations have found their way into modern, scholarly editions of Bach's works—for example the Bärenreiter edition of the *St. Matthew Passion* uses the Drinker translation. According to the *American Grove*'s biographer, Drinker's translations are "remarkable for their consistent craftsmanship, faithful prosody, and sheer number." Unfortunately, these translations are not easily accessible as they are long out of print. One can find them in some music libraries (see the listing beginning on p. 62) but in addition, some of Drinker's translations are found in modern editions.

While Drinker may be the most widely known personality in this field, there are some more modern editions that can aid in the understanding of the cantata texts. One source is *The Lutheran Chorales in the Organ Works of Bach* by Mark Bighley (Concordia, 1986). He has worked hard to create new, literal translations of the chorale texts, which can be carried over into the cantatas. He believes that any metrical translation must inevitably vary from the original meaning in order to maintain meter and rhyme patterns (see p. 3-7 of Bighley's book which describes this in more detail). A source that may be helpful is Charles Sanford Terry's *The Four-Part Chorales of J.S. Bach with the German Text of the Hymns and English Translations*, published by Oxford University Press, 1929. A more modern one is a book compiling all the cantata translations accompanying the complete recordings of Helmuth Rilling, published by Hännsler.

Ultimately, the idea of an English translation is still a compromise to some degree. Nevertheless, communication of the meanings of the cantata texts is still the primary goal and there are different ways to achieve this. Perhaps singing in English can be the stepping stone to learning the original German; good, pure vowels are needed in any language! But if singing in English moves the performer and especially the listener to understand Bach's intentions, then it will have served its purpose well.

An Annotated Bibliography of Sources on J.S. Bach

(with an emphasis on the vocal works)

Dr. David H. Chalmers

This bibliography is prepared as a guide to books that illuminate the works of J.S. Bach, particularly the sacred choral works. Each of these books is helpful to some degree in researching various aspects of Bach's life and works. The sources listed are in English unless otherwise noted.

Bettmann, Otto L. *Johann Sebastian Bach As His World Knew Him*, Birch Lane Press, 1995.
> A very interesting book, written by the founder of the Bettmann Archives. Arranged by subject, these personal essays reveal aspects of Bach's personal life in a fresh way.

Bighley, Mark S. *The Lutheran Chorales in the Organ Works of J.S. Bach*, Concordia Publishing House, 1986.
> A listing of the chorales contained in the organ works, but many of these are included in the vocal works. Gives English translations and much helpful commentary.

Boyd, Malcolm. *Bach, (Master Musician Series)*, 1983, Re-issued, Simon & Schuster, 1997.
> Originally published by J.M. Dent, this is a concise biography and contains further bibliographical information. Probably the best one volume biography of Bach.

Brown, Howard Mayer, ed. *Performance Practice-Music After 1600*, W.W. Norton, 1989.
> Part I (chapters 1-9) covers the Baroque era. All the commentary is extremely well documented and the chapter on voices in the Baroque is helpful.

Bullock, William J. *Bach Cantatas Requiring Limited Resources*, University Press of America, 1984.

This helpful book is a guide to the less difficult cantatas. The pieces are chronicled in outline form and much detail is given regarding instrumentation, voicings, and editions. This book would serve as a point of departure for those seeking a place to begin with the vocal works of Bach.

Butt, John. *Bach Interpretation*, Cambridge University Press, 1990.

This most thorough study of the articulation marks in Bach's works also contains an excellent chapter on the primacy of singing in interpreting Bach.

_____. *Bach-Mass in B Minor*, Cambridge University Press, 1991.

This is an excellent handbook on the genesis, history, and structure of the Mass. Helpful chapters include those on early performances, the dance influence, and structures. Much of this information can also be related to the *St. Matthew Passion*.

_____. *Music Education and the Art of Performance in the German Baroque*, Cambridge University Press, 1994.

A great deal of information on the educational and performance background of the age—one of the most extensive studies of its kind.

Butt, John, ed. *The Cambridge Companion to Bach*, Cambridge University Press, 1997.

Many useful articles, including two by Robin Leaver on the background of Lutheranism and the theological background of Bach as well as the function of the cantatas and choral works.

Chafe, Eric. *Tonal Allegory in the Vocal Music of J.S. Bach*, University of California Press, 1991.

A must for the serious study of Bach's sacred music. Describes the "spin" on the texts that Bach's music provides, i.e., music as allegory. Delves deeply into the musical and theological interpretation of the text.

David, Hans and Mendel, Arthur. *The Bach Reader*, W. W. Norton, 1966.

A classic compilation of letters and documents, many in Bach's own writing, that is fascinating reading and reveals much about Bach, the man. See especially Bach's "Short but Most Necessary Draft for Well-Appointed Church Music."

Dreyfus, Laurence. *Bach's Basso Continuo Group: Studies in the Performance of His Vocal Works*, Harvard University Press, 1987.

This important work explains the use of instruments in the continuo group for Bach's vocal works. It gives much original source material to enhance the ideas given about authenticity in Bach's continuo sound. The book contains a helpful catalog of original performance parts for Bach's vocal works.

Dürr, Alfred. *Die Kantaten von Johann Sebastian Bach*, Kassell, 1971, 4th reprint, 1981.

The best general study of the cantatas, though in German only.

Harnoncourt, Nikolaus. *Baroque Music Today: Music as Speech*, Amadeus Press, 1988.

This book contains much general information on interpretation in the Baroque with an historical context. The first two chapters are probably the most useful. Information applicable to Bach is spread throughout this thought-provoking book by a great interpreter of Bach's choral works.

Herz, Gerhard. *Essays on J.S. Bach*, U.M.I. Research Press, 1985.

Contains an interesting chapter on the *St. Matthew Passion* with a comparison of a similar work by another contemporary of Bach, Carl Heinrich Graun.

Irwin, J.H. *Neither Voice nor Heart Alone: German Lutheran Theology of Music in the Age of the Baroque*, Peter Lane Publishing, 1993.

A very well reasoned explanation of the function of music in a liturgical environment. Contentious, but informative.

Kavanaugh, Patrick. *The Spiritual Lives of Great Composers*, Sparrow Press, 1992

A marvelous book which contains a concise overview of Bach's spiritual life and thoughts. Very much worth reading as there are few books on music with such an emphasis on spirituality.

Leaver, Robin. *J.S. Bach and Scripture*, Concordia Publishing House, 1985.

This is an interesting book containing facsimile copies of annotations in Bach's own Bible. These annotations are very revealing of Bach's inner thinking and convictions and his Christian faith.

Marshall, Robert L. *The Music of Johann Sebastian Bach-The Sources, the Style, the Significance*, Schirmer Books, 1989.
    One of the finest comprehensive studies of Bach's work and life, this volume contains chapters on the vocal works, including a study of the origin of the *Magnificat.*

Melamed, Daniel R., ed. *Bach Studies 2*, Cambridge University Press, 1995.
    One of the most recent of scholarly books, there is a fascinating essay on the choral movements of the *St. Matthew Passion* by Ulrich Leisinger as well as articles by noted Bach scholars John Butt and Christoph Wolff.

Melamed, Daniel R. *J.S. Bach and the German Motet*, Cambridge University Press, 1995.
    This book defines the motet in the age of Bach and its liturgical-musical context. It gives much background on the composition of Bach's motets and their purpose.

Neumann, Frederick. *Ornamentation in Baroque and Post-Baroque Music*, Princeton University Press, 1983.
    Superbly researched and the most comprehensive book on ornamentation in the English language. There are specific chapters on Bach's ornaments.

Neumann, Werner. *Handbook of J.S. Bach's Cantatas*, Breitkopf und Härtel, 1971.
    Although in German, this is indispensable for finding all the pertinent musical information for each cantata. The cantatas are broken down by movements and keys, vocal ranges, instrumentation and other details are listed. One does not need an extensive knowledge of German to get a great deal of information from this book.

Quantz, J.J. *On Playing the Flute (1752)*, Free Press, 1966.
    Excellent treatise written in the 18th century on ornamentation and performance practice. Particularly interesting is Chapter 11: "Of Good Execution in General in Singing and Playing."

Schweitzer, Albert. *J.S. Bach*, Dover Publications, 1966.
    A more compact and accessible biography than the Spitta listed below. The 2nd volume contains a chapter on the *St. Matthew Passion.* There is much useful information on Bach's choral works, and Schweitzer emphasizes the spiritual aspect of Bach's work.

Smend, Friedrich. *Bach in Köthen*, Concordia Publishing House, 1985.
A comprehensive book on the middle period of Bach's life. Contains information on the *St. John Passion* and chapters 15-17 have interesting information on Bach's "Lutheranism" and the *secular* vs. the *sacred*.

Spitta, Philipp. *Johann Sebastian Bach*, Dover Publications, 1952.
The standard biography, written in the late nineteenth century. Book V, Chapter 7 discusses the *Passions*. This huge book contains many thorough descriptions and discussions of all of Bach's works.

Steinitz, Paul. *Performing Bach's Vocal Music*, Addington Press, 1980.
This is a helpful guide to much of the information needed to perform the sacred works of Bach. Particularly helpful are the suggestions for rehearsals, conducting, and obtaining performance materials. Much information is presented here in a compact format.

Stiller, Günther. *J.S. Bach and Liturgical Life in Leipzig*, Concordia Publishing House, 1984.
A thorough book on Bach's relationship to the worship life in Leipzig. There is much information on the liturgy of Bach's time including some references to the *Passions*.

Tatlow, Ruth. *Bach and the Riddle of the Number Alphabet*, Cambridge University Press, 1991.
Ms. Tatlow takes the symbolic numerology theories and debunks them in a fascinating study.

Webber, Geoffrey. *North German Church Music in the Age of Buxtehude*, Oxford University Press, 1996.
A very good general survey of sacred music in the period immediately before Bach.

Williams, Peter. *The Organ Music of J.S. Bach*, Vol 3—A Background, Cambridge University Press, 1984.
This particular volume contains a copious amount of information about the liturgy of Bach's day as well as much other valuable contextual information concerning Bach's sacred music in general.

Wolff, Christoph. *Bach—Essays on His Life and Music*, Harvard University Press, 1993.
A broad list of topics are covered here by a leading Bach scholar of today. Chapters 11, 12, and 30–32 about his vocal music are particularly interesting.

Library Resource Listings

The following information is a listing of some available English translations of Bach texts and many libraries from which they may be borrowed. Please contact your local public library or college or university library for more information on how to obtain these materials. At the time of writing of this handbook, all of the translations listed here are available through Inter-Library Loan from the libraries indicated.

Whittaker, William Gillies, *The cantatas of Johann Sebastian Bach: sacred and secular.* London: Oxford University, 1978.

New York
Library sigla
R   Eastman School of Music, Sibley Music Library

Bach, Johann Sebastian, 1685-1750. *Handbook to Bach's sacred cantata texts: an interlinear translation with reference guide to Biblical quotations and allusions.* Lanham, Maryland: Scarecrow Press, 1996. Unger, Melvin P., translator.

New York
Library sigla
BNG   State University of New York, Binghamton library
BUF   SUNY at Buffalo
COO   Cornell University
R   Eastman School of Music, Sibley Music Library
VJA   Adelphi University

VVP	Bard College
YSM	SUNY at Stony Brook
ZCU	Columbia University
ZJS	Juilliard School, The
ZMS	Manhattan School of Music
ZWU	Union College

Terry, Charles Sanford, 1864-1936. *Johann Sebastian Bach: cantata texts, sacred and secular, with a reconstruction of the Leipzig liturgy of his period.* London: Holland Press.

New York
Library sigla

BNY	New York Public Library
VZS	Skidmore College
XQM	Queens College

California
Library sigla

CRU	University of California, Riverside
SJP	San Jose Public Library
UOP	University of the Pacific

Iowa
Library sigla

ION	Coe College

Kansas
Library sigla

KTP	Topeka & Shawnee County Public Library

Massachusetts
Library sigla

WZW	Worcester Public Library

Minnesota
Library sigla

MHA	Hamline University

Missouri
Library sigla

MNW	Northwest Missouri State University
UMK	University of Missouri, Kansas City

North Carolina
Library sigla
NVS   Southeastern Baptist Theological Seminary

Nebraska
Library sigla
NBH   Hastings College

Ohio
Library sigla
YNG   Youngstown State University

Rhode Island
Library sigla
RIU   University of Rhode Island

Texas
Library sigla
IAU   Austin College

Virginia
Library sigla
VCB   Regent University
VRA   Radford University

Bach, Johann Sebastian. *Texts of the choral works of Johann Sebastian Bach in English translations*. New York: Print. priv. and distributed by the Association of American Colleges. Drinker, Henry Sandwith, tr.

New York
Texts of the choral works
Library sigla
SYB   Syracuse University
VVC   Colgate University
VVP   Bard College
VYE   Manhattanville College Library
XFM   SUNY College at Fredonia
YAH   Alfred University
YHM   Hamilton College Library
ZCU   Columbia University
ZIH   Hofstra University
ZTM   Mid-York Library System

Texte zu den Kirchenkantaten von Johann Sebastian Bach. The texts to Johann Sebastian Back's church cantatas. Neuhausen-Stuttgart, Hänssler-Verlag, 1984. Translation by Z. Philip Ambrose.

New York
Library sigla
BNG   State University of New York, Binghamton Library
BNY   New York Public Library
COO   Cornell University
NYP   New York Public Library Resource Library
R   Eastman School of Music, Sibley Music Library
VVS   Sarah Lawrence College
XNC   Nazareth College
YPM   SUNY College at Plattsburgh
YSM   SUNY at Stony Brook
ZCU   Columbia University
ZGM   CUNY Graduate School
ZJS   Juilliard School, The
ZWU   Union College

Bach, Johann Sebastian, *Die Bach Kantate.* Recording. 100 sound discs in 10 v. All the church cantatas. *Texte zu den Kirchenkantaten von Johann Sebastian Bach*—The texts of Johann Sebastian Bach's church cantatas, translated by Z. Philip Ambrose (491 pp.), accompanying recordings.
(These recordings are listed because translations are available in the liner notes)

Louisiana
Library sigla
LWA   University of Southwestern Louisiana

Massachusetts
Library sigla
ENG   New England Conservatory of Music

Minnesota
Library sigla
MNC   Concordia College

Utah
Library sigla
UBY   Brigham Young University Library

Alabama
Library sigla
ALM   University of Alabama

California
Library sigla
CSL   University of Southern California

Georgia
Library sigla
GMU   Mercer University, Main Library

Minnesota
Library sigla
MST   Saint Cloud State University

Missouri
Library sigla
MUU   University of Missouri, Columbia
MWS   Missouri Western State College

Nebraska
Library sigla
LDL   University of Nebraska at Lincoln

Ohio
Library sigla
OBE   Oberlin College

Pennsylvania
Library sigla
DKC   Dickinson College
PGM   Messiah College Learning Center
UPM   Pennsylvania State University

Rhode Island
Library sigla
RBN   Brown University

Virginia
Library sigla
VLB   Liberty University

Wisconsin
Library sigla
WOP   Edgewood College, Oscar Rennebohm Library
WRO   Wisconsin Lutheran College Library

Canada
Library sigla
UWO   University of Western Ontario